15 Easy Folktale Fingerplays

With Cross-Curricular Activities

by Bill Gordh

SCHOLASTIC
PROFESSIONAL BOOKS

NEW YORK • TORONTO • LONDON • AUCKLAND • SYDNEY

For my wife, Jenny, and children, Cody and Rachel, who hear all my stories; and to the Episcopal School of New York City, where these fingerplays were developed.

Cover design and illustration by Viv Eisner-Hess
Cover type treatment by Jaime Lucero
Interior design by Kathy Massaro
Interior illustrations by James Hale and Larry Daste
Activities edited by Mary Beth Spann
Copy editor: Jeannie Hutchins

ISBN: 0-590-96392-9
Copyright © 1997 by Bill Gordh
All rights reserved.
Printed in the U.S.A.

12 11 10 9 8 7 6 5 4 3 2 1   7 8 9/9/01/0

Contents

Introduction

Folktales are a part of the oral tradition of every culture. They have been told and retold to enchant, involve, and provoke listeners. They have evolved according to both the culture they are told in and the age and number of the listeners. These tales have been told in order to be retold again and again, and as a result are often structured in a way that makes them easy to remember. Retelling these stories as fingerplays takes this idea one step further. By giving children hand movements to accompany the stories, they become more fully involved. They are participating in the story itself by physically experiencing its structure, action, and characters. Just as manipulatives are helpful to young mathematicians, these gestures give children a way to hold on to the stories. The body helps the mind remember, and the stories become the children's own.

How to Use This Book

The 15 stories in this collection represent many cultures from around the world. I have selected and adapted them specifically for the fingerplay approach. Your class will enjoy the stories even without the fingerplay gestures. However, with the gestures, you have an opportunity to engage your children in a very exciting story adventure.

The sequence of stories is based on the ease of sharing the fingerplay gestures with your class. However, if you are drawn to a story that appears later in the book, or fits your curriculum now, by all means use it!

Kinds of Fingerplays

★ Some fingerplays represent characters: The shape and movement of the hand and fingers represent different characters, such as Spider or Rabbit or Sun.

★ Some fingerplays depict the reader or storyteller as a character: In *The Tomorrow Monkeys* and *The Stonecutter*, the storyteller becomes a character, while the hands represent other elements in the story.

★ Some fingerplays describe movement: Rain falling (fingers wiggling downward), or characters walking (hands patting thighs), are examples of this kind of fingerplay. Sometimes fingerplays describe the action of the characters rather than the characters themselves. For example, in *Sparrow and Crow*, the sparrow asks the woodcutter to chop down the tree. Instead of representing the woodcutter as a finger character, the fingerplay suggests his action, chopping.

Tips for Getting Started

The stories have been set up so that you do not really "teach" them, in the sense of sitting down and going over the gestures beforehand and practicing them. As I have discovered from years of storytelling, the fingerplays are naturally inviting to children. They can't wait to participate! At times, as you get farther into the book, the sequence of gestures may be harder to remember, but even then this can be a fun challenge for children. Here are more tips for sharing the tales with children:

★ Each story offers start-up ideas for setting the stage for the fingerplay, including a suggested motivation for children to listen carefully to the story about to be told. If you wish, you may also introduce each story by talking with children about similar books or stories they are familiar with. That way, you can determine if children are already acquainted with the vocabulary you are about to share in the story.

★ On your own, read the story aloud a couple of times before sharing it with your class. Practice the fingerplays so that you can be a model.

★ Introduce the book to the class. You might say something like, "I have some new stories to share with you. They include fingerplays or hand plays (older children might respond more to the term hand plays). We can tell them together!"

After the first session, children will understand the idea of the fingerplays, and will be ready every time you bring out the book.

★ Introduce the first character or action to the class before you start the story. You might say, "This story has a spider in it. Let's make a spider!" Allow a little time for the children to explore the movement of this character. You might ask a few children to show a movement and ask other children to copy it.

★ Begin reading the story. Invite children to copy your fingerplay demonstration of the first character when it is introduced. When a new action or character appears, the children will be watching and will copy your move. If you notice someone not quite following, keep the story moving so that you do not interrupt its flow. The challenge and fun of doing the gestures involve children and they will want to do the same story over and over. As the story and fingerplays are repeated, children will pick up things they missed the first time. Repetition also helps the gestures become more fluid for everyone. Of course you will not want to limit yourself to the finger movements suggested in this book—please feel free to develop movements of your own, and invite children to do the same! (See the ideas that follow.)

Expanding the Fingerplays

The fingerplay suggestions that accompany each story cover the story's basic outline. Once children have mastered these fingerplay gestures, they will be eager to innovate on them, or add fingerplays to other aspects of the tale. For example, in *The Tomorrow Monkeys*, the fingerplays follow the lives of the monkeys. You can devise fingerplays to show the sun setting, wind blowing, or rain coming down. These additions make the sequences even more visual. Here are some additional ideas for expanding the fingerplays:

★ Encourage children to make up additional characters, adventures, and other descriptive details such as facial expressions to enhance the story's visual appeal.

★ Invite children to turn the fingerplays into puppet plays. Children can draw simple characters on construction paper and glue these to craft sticks.

★ Consider presenting a few fingerplays for an audience. You might use a tape of classical music to set the story mood and offer groups of students parts to recite together to bring a "readers' theater" feel to your performance.

★ Help children find other stories that can be adapted into fingerplays or puppet plays. Consider having children write and perform simple songs to enhance their performances. (Tip: Rely on well-known tunes and then just substitute new lyrics for the standard.)

★ Whenever possible, turn the play into a book complete with illustrations, or a mural complete with dialogue balloons. This practice offers children important writing experience, while reinforcing for children their awareness of each story's unique structure.

Across the Curriculum

You can easily extend these stories across your curriculum. Following each story are activities that connect the stories to language arts, science, social studies, math, dramatic play, art, and other aspects of your class's curriculum. Here are some additional ideas that you can use with all of the stories in this book:

★ Invite students to retell the story in their own words. As is suggested throughout the book, you can write down their versions of the story and then have them add illustrations. Arrange each student's version on a single sheet of oak tag or chart paper. Children can present them as gifts to special people or as thank-you's to classroom volunteers.

★ Suggest to students that they collect favorite family stories, write them down and present them as fingerplays. For example, maybe they can tell the story of the time "Grandpa Took Us to Get Pizza" or the time "Aunt Bessie Tried out

My Bicycle." When helping students polish their stories, you can help them look for places where repetition and movements come in naturally. ("And then Grandpa drove up and drove down and drove up and drove down and drove up and drove down until we arrived at Pizza Palace.")

★ Collect folktales from around the world. How many places and peoples can you represent with stories?

Using the Audiocassette

I have recorded these 15 stories on an accompanying audiocassette to lend support to and further appreciation of this book. (The cassette is sold separately, ISBN: 0-590-96401-1.) The stories have been told at a pace which provides maximum listening enjoyment.

★ Practice the fingerplays in the story at least once without the tape.

★ Before listening to the story on the tape, review the gestures with children.

★ Once children have mastered the fingerplays, they will enjoy doing them on their own while listening to the stories on the tape at a learning center. The musical accompaniments to many of the stories may suggest ways for children to innovate on the characters' movements.

★ Divide the class into groups so that each group has all the characters in a particular story. Each group can act out the story as they listen to it on the tape.

★ Offer children the opportunity to take the tape home and play it for their families. Place the tape plus a copy of the fingerplay story in a self-closing plastic bag. Include also a small blank notebook so families can offer feedback on the experience.

★ Use the tape to help support class performances of the fingerplays. Children can also use the tape to help teach the stories and movements to their schoolmates.

I hope that you find these fingerplay stories as valuable as I have. Over the years, I have told many, many folktales, using a variety of approaches. Fingerplays provide an exciting enhancement to the listening experience, and the involvement of children is gratifying. I have been astounded at children's recall of both the story and its fingerplays after just one telling! I hope you and your class enjoy this "hands-on" approach to storytelling.

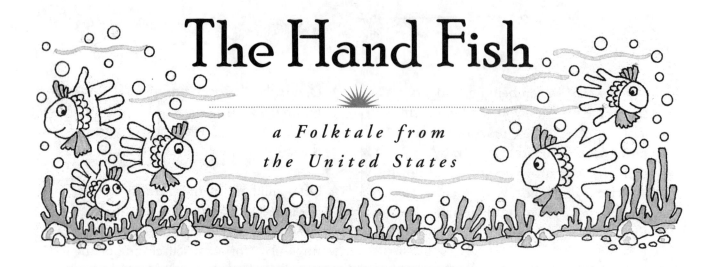

The Hand Fish

*a Folktale from
the United States*

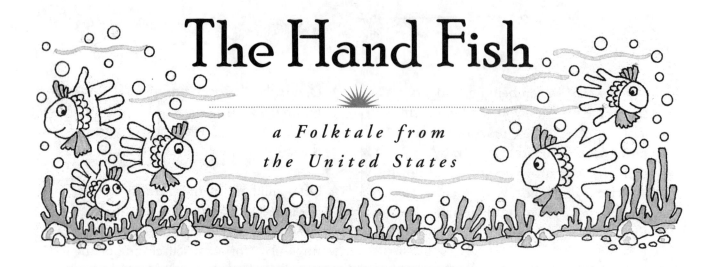

American folklore is filled with tall tales of humorous, fantastical animals such as Paul Bunyan's big blue ox, Babe. Others include a dog that walks backward; and an animal that walks sideways on hillsides because the legs on one side of its body are longer than the other. A walking catfish and a hairy fish are other kinds of tall-tale fish.

Fingerplay Start-Ups

Tell the children that they are going to hear a story about a type of fish called a "Hand Fish." Ask if they can imagine why a fish might be called by this unusual name. Jot down children's ideas on the chalkboard or on a piece of chart paper. Then tell them to listen carefully to discover if they guessed the meaning behind the name.

You may have never heard of Hand Fish but there used to be lots of them swimming the rivers and streams of America.

They were amazing animals and were called Hand Fish because they looked exactly like hands. They had some unusual habits.

One was that they always **swam thumbs up** in the morning and **thumbs down** in the afternoon.

In the evening they would **swim palms up** and when they slept they would still swim, but always **palms down**. That was the best time to catch them.

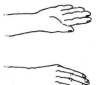

People always said that if you saw a Hand Fish palm down you knew it was asleep and if you could slip a black glove on it just before it woke up, you had it.

The folks that did catch them were usually quick and were often jokers, so sometimes at a party you might wind up **shaking hands with a Hand Fish** instead of a real hand!

Another thing that was quite remarkable about Hand Fish was how they worked in pairs. If a Hand Fish got hungry, it would go and **grab some little fish**, like a baby trout, and **throw it to its partner. The partner would catch it and throw it back into the first Hand Fish's mouth**—kind of like baseball.

They loved watching one another do this, so you would often see and hear pairs of **Hand Fish clapping for one another.**

Now with all these skills you would think that Hand Fish would still be around. But there are still people talking about that sad day way back when, when they waved good-bye to the last of the Hand Fish.

The good-bye story goes like this.

Everything was going great for the Hand Fish until the Feet Fish showed up. Now the Feet Fish and the Hand Fish were not enemies, as you might think, but their habits did not work well together.

You see, the Feet Fish traveled on the bottom of the rivers and **their stomping** stirred up so much mud and dirt that **the Hand Fish couldn't keep a grip on anything**. When they lost that grip, they couldn't hold on to any food, and it was time to move on.

So the Hand Fish took off. Just picture it. People lined up along the river banks waving good-bye, and those **Hand Fish jumping out of the water waving good-bye right back**. It was a sad day.

Where they went no one is quite sure, though there is at least one report of a sighting out at sea. It seems a school of Hand Fish was swimming by a ship, when the order rang out, "All hands on deck!" The next thing they knew, the ship's crew had a deck full of Hand Fish!

I'm not sure that last story is really true, but it seems now you hardly ever hear of anyone seeing any Hand Fish. I sure hope they're okay.

THE END

Talking About the Story

Ask children why they think this story is called a tall tale. (It stretches or exaggerates the truth.) Have children decide on some things in the story they think could have happened (fish swim in the river) and some things that were too silly or outrageous to have really happened (when the Hand Fish got hungry they would throw baby trout back and forth). You might consider reading the story aloud slowly and asking children to raise their hands when you come to an example that makes the story a tall tale.

Across the Curriculum

CONSTRUCTING TALL TALES
Language Arts

Have children research the habits and behaviors of different kinds of fish. Then help them to choose a "real-life" fish to feature in an original tall-tale fish story. Help the children understand that one way to construct a tall tale is to consider the animal's natural attributes and then weave in powerful, unusual, or human attributes. For example, they might make up a story about a rainbow fish able to jump out of the fish bowl in search of the end of the rainbow, or a goldfish able to turn things into gold. For youngest storytellers, you may want to describe a character and begin telling a story

involving the character, and then ask the children to take turns adding on story segments. Tape-record your efforts so you can enjoy your class's tall tales again and again.

PAPER HAND FISH AND FEET FISH
Art and Math

Have children trace their hands (with fingers closed) and stocking feet onto different-colored pieces of construction paper. Then have them cut out the shapes. Offer children materials so they may decorate their fish to look as magical as possible. Then use children's creations in the following activities:

★ **Aquarium Bulletin Board:** Invite children to display their creations on a bulletin board covered with blue craft paper. If you like, cover the display with clear or light-blue cellophane to simulate a real underwater scene.

★ **Hand-and-Feet-Fish Math:** Have children use the Hand Fish and Feet Fish to do some classroom estimation and measurement. For example: How many Hand Fish high is your desk? Find something in the classroom that is as wide as two Feet Fish. How many Hand Fish and Feet Fish, placed end-to-end, would we need to make a fish chain that stretches from our door to the principal's office?

The Frog Pond

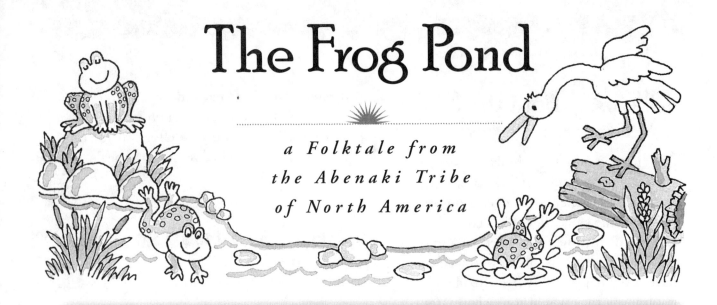

a Folktale from the Abenaki Tribe of North America

This story is a satirical commentary on the importance of choosing a leader wisely. There is a similar fable, told during the Middle Ages in France, of a group of pigeons who chose a hawk for their king. What happened? The pigeons were eaten by their leader!

Fingerplay Start-Ups

Introduce the story by asking for volunteers to act out the parts of the frogs. Then introduce the frog gesture, allowing time for the participants to practice. Also, consider asking for volunteers to play the parts of the log and the crane, or play these roles yourself.

Once there was a frog pond out in the woods. **It was full of frogs**—some on rocks, some on lily pads, and some in the water with their big eyes just above the surface.

The frogs led a very happy life. **Their chief was an old log** which lay at one end of the pond. It never bothered them and there was always plenty to eat.

Then one day **a large white bird flew down** and

landed in the shallow water. It had long legs. It had white feathers and **a long graceful neck**. The frogs had never before seen anything so beautiful.

They looked at this beautiful new creature. Then they looked across the pond at their chief, the old log. The log was not beautiful at all.

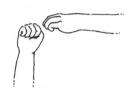

The frogs decided that they should make the bird their chief. They chose one frog to carry their message.

The frog hopped over to the bird. The large bird looked down at the little frog. "We would like you to be our chief!" called the frog. **The bird nodded her fine white head.**

The frogs were so excited that they started hopping to celebrate. Some hopped on their old chief, the log. Others hopped rock to rock and onto the pond's bank. Night settled in and the frogs sang for their new chief.

The next morning, there was silence at that frog pond. Why was it silent? Because there were no more frogs. Why? **Because their new chief had eaten up every one of them.**

T H E   E N D

Talking About the Story

Discuss with children why they think the frogs chose the bird for their leader, and why the bird agreed so easily. Ask: If you were a frog, who would you pick for a leader? Would you choose another frog? If so, which frog would you pick? The highest jumper? The one with the longest tongue? What qualities would a good frog leader need?

Across the Curriculum

LITERATURE LINKS
Language Arts

Share other stories about characters who are judged (favorably or unfavorably) on the basis of their looks. Perhaps students can recount the story of *Beauty and the Beast*, *The Ugly Duckling* or *Snow White and the Seven Dwarfs* (in which Snow White is fooled into trusting the witch who is disguised as an old peddler). Talk together about why traditionally beautiful-looking characters are thought to be beautiful inside, and why characters who are not good looking (like the Beast in *Beauty and the Beast*) are thought to be not good on the inside. Ask: Is it ever possible to know all about someone just by looking at them on the outside? Do you know and love anyone who is not really beautiful looking on the outside? Talk also about the phrase "love is blind," and explain that it means that when you do love someone, his or her looks are less important than what's inside.

FACT OR FICTION?
Language Arts and Science

Ask children if they believe this story could really have happened. Why or why not? Guide children to understand that while it is not likely that frogs would choose to follow a log or a bird, many animal species do choose one of their own to lead the rest. Research different kinds of animals to determine if and how they choose leaders.

FOLLOW-THE-LEADER
Movement

Supply some snappy music and invite children to take turns leading the group in some movement activity (dancing, hopping, stretching, tapping, turning, bending, etc.). If classroom space is at a premium, you may want to limit movement possibilities to in-place movements. After everyone who wants to be the leader has had a chance to do so, talk with children about what being the leader felt like. Also, remind children that it's okay if they don't always feel comfortable being in a leader role.

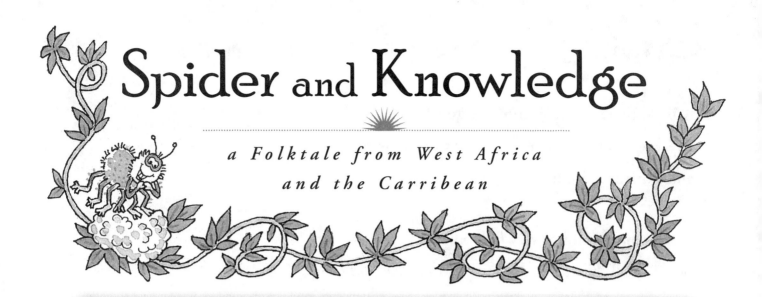

Spider and Knowledge

*a Folktale from West Africa
and the Carribean*

In this tale, Spider tries to collect all the knowledge in the world and keep it for himself. Needless to say, this is not possible, even for Spider.

Fingerplay Start-Ups

Before beginning this story, introduce the hand gesture that represents the gourd.

Explain that a gourd is a fruit with a rounded shape similar to that of a pumpkin or squash. Some gourds, like the one in this story, are kept whole and used as jugs and rattles, while others are cut in half and used as dippers and bowls. Gourds are often decorated with carvings depicting animals or abstract designs. They are called calabashes.

Spider thought he knew everything! He looked around and said, "I am the smartest in the whole world! No one is as smart as I am. In fact, I think I'll gather up the few things I don't know, and then I'll have all the knowledge in the world!" He smiled at this thought.

Spider went to work. He took a big gourd, shaped kind of like a pumpkin, hollowed it out and fixed it up with a stopper. Then he started gathering knowledge.

A little here—stuff it into the gourd.

A little there—stuff it into the gourd.

Everywhere he went, he gathered more knowledge and stuffed it into his gourd.

Finally the gourd was very full. Spider smiled. He now had all the knowledge in the world! He pushed the stopper into the gourd, and looked around for a place to hide his treasure. He was not going to share it with anyone.

When he saw a palm tree, he knew he had found the perfect hiding place. He was so smart! **He took hold of the gourd, held it close to his belly and started climbing**. It was tricky going. Spider kept slipping with that gourd between him and the tree.

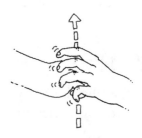

He heard some laughter from the bottom of the tree. He looked down. There were two of his children, a son and a daughter. He said, "What are you laughing about?"

They called back, "Carry the gourd on your back! It will be a lot easier."

Spider heard what they said and realized they were right. **He flipped the gourd over his shoulder and climbed easily up the rest of the tree.**

When he got to the top, he realized he had not gathered all the knowledge, for his very own children knew something he didn't know. This made him so angry that **he flung the gourd down to the ground.**

The gourd smashed into thousands of pieces, and knowledge scattered across the world.

That's why we all know something.

T H E   E N D

Talking About the Story

Talk about knowledge. You might ask: What are some things you know? How did you learn them? What is something everyone knows?

Across the Curriculum

STORING KNOWLEDGE
Social Studies

In the story, knowledge is stored in the gourd and is spread through the breaking of the gourd. Make a list with students of all the ways and places we store knowledge.

Make a second list of various ways knowledge travels around the world. (Tip: Tell students to think of places they go to learn information and ways they pass on what they learn.)

GOURD INVESTIGATIONS
Science

Gourds are used for many things—bowls, cups, and containers. If possible, obtain some gourds (often available at farm stands in the fall) and bring them into class. Pass them around and discuss their properties. Could these gourds be used as the one described in the story? Why or why not? If your collection includes dried gourds, try using these as natural rhythm instruments.

Inga and the 10 Fairy Helpers

Based on a Folktale from Sweden

This old Scandinavian tale follows a young girl's transformation from a "hands in her lap" person to an active and helpful child. Because the girl puts her fingers to work, the story is tailor-made for fingerplay interpretation!

Fingerplay Start-Ups

This tale includes many actions for children to pantomine. Before sharing the story with your class, make a list on chart paper of all the actions children could possibly act out. Share your list with children and encourage them to come up with unique gestures for each action. Tell them that they are to stand up to perform each action. But every time you read the line "Inga sat, hands in her lap," they should sit down (on chairs or on the floor) and fold their hands in their laps. To add to the fun, read the story slowly at the beginning to indicate Inga's initial inactivity, and then speed up your pace toward the end to match Inga's newly acquired energy.

Once there was a girl named Inga. Inga did not like to work! She was an only child and her parents did everything for her. What did Inga do? **Inga sat, hands in her lap**.

Her mother laced up Inga's shoes while **Inga sat, hands in her lap**.
Her father cleared the dinner table while **Inga sat, hands in her lap**.

All the work to be done was done
while **Inga sat, hands in her lap**.

Then, one summer, Inga went to stay with her cousins.
Her cousins did their share of the chores.
But even with their example,
Inga sat, hands in her lap.

But Inga's cousins did not tidy up her room.
Nor did they smooth the spread on her bed.
So Inga's room got very messy.
She didn't like it like that.
But still Inga sat, hands in her lap.

Sitting alone in her messy room, tears filled her eyes and
trickled down her cheeks. Suddenly, a strange little man
appeared. He told her that he was her fairy godfather.

"You don't like this messy room, but you don't want to
clean it up, is that right?" he asked.

Inga nodded.

"Well, here are ten little helpers to help you out!"
He snapped his fingers and **ten little fairies appeared.**
They went right to work and, in no time at all, the
room was spotless.

19

Inga was smiling!

Her fairy godfather said to Inga, **"Take your**
hands out of your lap." She did.
"Now stretch them out," he said. **She did.**

Now he spoke to the helpers,
"Thumb—Hop, Hop!"
And the first helper hopped into Inga's thumb.
"Now you, Old Pointer!"
And the next fairy jumped into her pointer finger.
"Stand tall, Tall One!"
And the third leapt into Inga's middle finger.
"Good Friend, go join her!"
This helper went into her ring finger.
"Little One, have fun, quickly now!"
And the fifth little helper leapt into Inga's little finger.

Her Fairy Godfather repeated his directions to the other
five helpers:
"Thumb—Hop, Hop!"
"Now you, Old Pointer!"
"Stand tall, Tall One!"
"Good Friend, go join her!"
"Little One, have fun, quickly now!"
And they leapt into Inga's other five fingers.

The Fairy Godfather added,

"I think that's all you need!"

And he disappeared.

And it was all she needed.

Inga's fingers felt so alive, they couldn't rest in her lap.

She wiggled them around.

They wanted to do something!

So Inga ran downstairs,

set the table,

and straightened the chairs;

cooked the dinner,

and swept the floor;

cleaned the dishes,

and painted the door;

tied her shoes,

and put the tools away.

Then she ran outside with her cousins to play.

And from that day on,

Inga never again sat,

with her hands in her lap.

T H E   E N D

Talking About the Story

How much children are expected to "pitch in" at home can vary greatly from household to household. The following questions are designed to help children explore this issue. Ask: What do you think about how Inga's parents acted when Inga sat with her hands in her lap? Do you think Inga's parents helped her by doing everything for her? Why or why not? Are you responsible for any chores at home? If so, how do you help out? Which chores do you enjoy the most? The least? Do you think it's important for kids to help out, or should they expect grown-ups to do all the work?

Across the Curriculum

FEEL THE BEAT
Movement

The last stanza of the story includes gestures that students can act out to a steady beat. Have children sit in a circle. Start a simple steady beat of clapping hands, then slapping thighs, then slapping thighs with crossed arms. Encourage children to join in. Then read the last stanza in time with the beat of the gestures. Take turns going around the circle. One at a time, each person adds to or changes the pattern of the gestures. Continue until everyone has had a chance to be the movement leader.

COUNTING ON FINGERS
Math

Challenge children to solve simple addition and subtraction finger problems inspired by the story movements. For example, you might ask:

★ If the fairies hopped only into Inga's thumbs, how many fingers would not have fairies? (8)

★ If the only fairies to hop into Inga's fingers were the fairies on her ring fingers and on her little fingers, how many fairies would be in Inga's fingers? (4)

★ If fairies hopped into Inga's two pointer fingers and into her two middle fingers, and then the fairies in the pointers hopped off again, how many fairies would be left in Inga's fingers? (2)

REBUS FUN
Language Arts

Use a large piece of chart paper to record the story's second-to-last verse (describing the housework Inga does with her fingers). Underline the nouns in the passage. Then provide children with removable sticky notes and invite them to turn the verse into a rebus story by drawing one illustration for each noun. (If you wish to add a bit of mystery to the activity, just ask each child to draw a specific picture, without telling them why you need it.) Cover each underlined word with a rebus picture. Then, read the passage together. Allow children time to take turns "reading" the picture, then lifting the flap to reveal the word beneath.

The Fly's Castle

a Folktale from Russia

Cumulative tales are constructed so that the same action is repeated by a series of characters until the story's climax. In this story, a series of animals are invited into the fly's castle. But the arrival of a clumsy bear creates chaotic results. Similar tales appear in many cultures. Other familiar Russian cumulative tales include *The Mitten* and *The Great Big Enormous Turnip*. Another old cumulative favorite is *The House That Jack Built*.

Fingerplay Start-Ups

In this story, the gestures begin with fingertip movements (representing the fly and the flea). As the story progresses, and as the animals that visit the fly's castle become progressively larger, the movements used to tell the story increase in size, too. Before sharing the selection, ask children to pay attention to the movements you model so they may later tell what they notice about how you use your body to help tell the story.

One day, **a fly** built her very own castle.

Along came a flea who asked,

"Who's in the castle?"

"I!" said the fly.

"Come on in!"

And the flea flew in.

Then along came a mouse who asked,

"Who's in the castle?"

"I!" said the fly;

"And me!" called the flea.

"Come on in!"

And the mouse crawled in.

Then along came a hare who asked,

"Who's in the castle?"

"I!" said the fly;

"And me!" called the flea;

"Me, too!" cried the mouse.

"Come on in!"

And the hare hopped in.

Then along came a fox who asked,

"Who's in the castle?"

"I!" said the fly;

"And me!" called the flea;

"Me, too!" cried the mouse;

"Ya-hoo!" said the hare.

"Come on in!"

And the fox leapt in.

Then along came a wolf who asked,

"Who's in the castle?"

"I!" said the fly;

"And me!" called the flea;

"Me, too!" cried the mouse;

"Ya-hoo!" said the hare;

"I'm here," cried the fox.

"Come on in!"

And the wolf went in.

Then along came a bungling bear who asked,

"Who's in the castle?"

"I!" said the fly;

"And me!" called the flea;

"Me, too!" cried the mouse;

"Ya-hoo!" said the hare;

"I'm here," cried the fox;

"Here, here," wailed the wolf.

"Come on in!"

But that great big bungling bear,

without even being aware,

with a swing of its paw

sent the castle and all

on a flight right up into the air!

THE END

Talking About the Story

Discuss the story ending. Ask children to tell what they believe is meant by the final sentence: "But that great big bungling bear, without even being aware, with a swing of its paw sent the castle and all on a flight right up into the air!"

Across the Curriculum

ANIMAL CARD GAMES
Math and Science

Paste or draw a picture of each animal on unruled index cards and label each with the animal's name. The pictures should reflect the animals' varying sizes. Then use the set of cards in the following activities:

★ Help children sort and classify the animal cards according to different attributes. Lay two large yarn circles on the floor. Have children take turns sorting the cards into two different groups (big/small animals, fur/no fur, insects/mammals, etc.). Challenge the other children to guess the sorting criteria.

★ In the story, each animal enters the castle according to its size. Invite students to sequence the animal cards according to animal size, from smallest to biggest.

HOW MUCH DOES IT HOLD?
Math and Science

This story involves the concept of volume. If possible, take your class to visit a few different elevators. Point out the sign that lists the elevators' passenger capacity. Ask: Why do you think this sign is here? How do you think inspectors decide on this number? Back in the classroom, hand out empty shoe boxes, and counters such as linking cubes. Tell students to pretend that the boxes are elevators and the counters are people. Ask them to estimate how many cubes they think the box will hold.

ACT IT OUT
Language Arts and Drama

Ask for volunteers to take turns playing the animals in the story. Then have children act out the story as you recite it. As you retell the story, each "animal" enters the castle (a designated spot marked off with masking tape on the floor) when its name is called and makes its fingerplay gesture. As more and more animals enter the castle, children will find the need to huddle closer and closer together to depict the close quarters. When the bear arrives and swipes its paw, children run in all directions, waving their arms.

The Clay Teapot Takes Charge

a Folktale from China

This humorous tale from China features a bossy teapot who, from her perch high up on a shelf, barks out orders to a needle, an onion, a fly, a mudpie, and some rice flour. Each character attempts to help with the household chores, but meets with disastrous results. Like *The Wild Cherry Tree* (page 54), this story relies on personification to bring its characters to life.

Fingerplay Start-Ups

Offer children modeling compound and have them use the material to fashion the objects that double as characters in the story (teapot, needle, onion, fly, mudpie, and rice flour). Then invite volunteers to use their clay characters to act out the story as the rest of the class provides fingerplay movements.

This story has no people.

But this story has a house.

And one day in this house, **the clay teapot took charge**.

Standing on the shelf, she called in her helpers:

Needle, Onion, Fly, Mudpie, and Rice Flour.

Then, she gave out the orders:

"Needle, sweep the floor!

Onion, bring the cow home!

Fly, herd in the ox!

Mudpie, fetch the water!

Rice Flour, check the weather!"

Then Clay Teapot sat up on the shelf waiting

for the work to be done.

Well, her friends tried; but this is what happened.

When Needle went to sweep the floor,

What happened?

It slipped and fell into a crack.

When Onion tried to lead the cow home,

What happened?

The cow was hungry and gobbled it up.

When Fly started to drive in the ox,

What happened?

With a swing of its tail, the ox sent the fly high into the clouds.

When Mudpie carried the bucket,

What happened?

Some of the water sloshed out and turned Mudpie into just

plain old mud.

And when Rice Flour climbed onto the roof

to check the weather,

What happened?

The wind blew it in a hundred different directions.

Now all this time the clay teapot was waiting patiently, but after waiting and waiting and waiting, she decided to see what was going on.

So Clay Teapot jumped off the shelf to the ground.

What happened?

She had forgotten she was made of clay, and **she shattered into thousands of little pieces.**

It was a bad luck day for that household!

THE END

Talking About the Story

Ask children to describe the chores they participate in at home. Ask: Are there any jobs you aren't allowed to help with at this time? Why?

Across the Curriculum

WORKING TOGETHER
Social Studies

Have children brainstorm a list of jobs requiring a variety of workers, plus a list of workers for each job. For example, building a house might require the help of carpenters, plumbers, electricians, and roofers. Have children remember times they worked with others to get a job done. Was it easy or hard? Find out which students prefer working alone and which ones prefer working in cooperation with others.

ILLUSTRATED BIG BOOK
Language Arts

Invite children to retell this story to you. Write their version of the story on a large sheet of chart paper. Reprint the words to each scene at the bottom of a piece of white oak tag. Then divide the story scenes so that pairs or small groups of students can work together to illustrate one scene on the oak tag. Assemble the book and share it with the whole class.

The Honey Pot

a Folktale from the Middle East

The moral of this story is "every little bit counts!" When the townspeople in a small village plan to present their king with a splendid birthday gift, they discover the importance of each individual's contribution to a group effort. The tale also touches upon themes involving sharing things that are precious and the importance of cooperation.

Fingerplay Start-Ups

Tell children that in this story, the villagers are planning a surprise for their king—but that in the end, they get the biggest surprise of all! Ask children to listen carefully to see if they can figure out the surprise ending.

A long time ago, there lived a king in a small village. His birthday was coming soon and everyone in the village was talking about it.

But what should they give their King?

A man suggested, "How about a horse?"

They all shook their heads.

No, the King had the most beautiful horses in the land.

A woman called out, "How about a goat?
It will bring the King's family milk and cheese."
They all shook their heads.
The King had hundreds of goats already.

"How about honey?"
asked a girl named Noora.

"Honey?!" said everyone. "Why honey?"

"Well," replied Noora, "The King loves honey, and
if each of us gave a cup, we could fill a huge pot, and
it would last him for years and years."

**The rest of the townspeople looked at one another
and started smiling and nodding.** They liked this idea!

The people dragged a huge pot to the center of the
village. Then everyone went home to get their cups
of honey.

When Noora got home, **she opened her cupboard
and got out her cup. Then she took out her little
pot of honey.** Oh, how Noora loved honey! In fact she
loved honey so much she did not want to give any of it
away. She thought about it.

There were many people in her village. Each person would pour a cup of honey into the big pot.

Noora got an idea. If she put water in her cup instead of honey, no one would ever know. The King certainly wouldn't notice a little water in all of that honey!

Noora quickly put her little honey pot back on the shelf and **filled her cup with water**.

Then she went with her cup and stood in line with everyone else. Noora watched as one by one, the villagers emptied their cups into the great pot. Now it was Noora's turn. **She emptied her cup into the pot, too**.

Then the villagers invited the King to come and see his birthday present.

The King arrived. He looked at the full pot in front of him. He looked out across the crowd. They all shouted, "It's honey!" He smiled, **dipped his finger into the pot** and **took a taste**.

He looked up with a strange expression on his face.

"Is this a joke?" he asked.

The people shook their heads. The King cried, "This pot is full of water!"

All the villagers stared at their King.

What could have happened? Can you guess? Well if you guessed that all the villagers had the same idea as the young girl, Noora, you would be right. Everyone in the village had filled their cups with water, too!

THE END

Talking About the Story

Talk with children about sharing. Help them conclude that some things are easy to share, while it's harder to share or give away special things. Ask: What do you do when adults expect you to share but you don't want to? Can you talk about any special sharing rules in place at your home?

Across the Curriculum

HONEY AND WATER
Science

Here are several different ideas to help students explore and experiment with water and honey:

★ Have students use their senses to make a chart listing the properties of both honey and water according to various criteria (taste, smell, color, texture, thickness,

pourability, etc.). Have samples of honey and water on hand so students can conduct mini-experiments to compare how the two are alike and how they are different.

★ Help children find out how honey is made. Also discover together why honey is so precious, and consequently so expensive. (To make just one jar of honey, bees make about two million trips to flowers!)

★ Have a Honey-Tasting Party: Invite students to taste and compare different kinds of honey such as orange blossom, buckwheat, alfalfa, clover, and tupelo.

★ Ask: If everyone except Noora had put in honey, would her trick have worked? How can we find out? Mix honey and water to discover what happens.

COOPERATIVE MEASUREMENT
Math and Science

Invite children to investigate how many cups of water it would take to fill the King's pot. You will need a large plastic tub and one small paper cup per child. Have children estimate how many cups full of water they believe it will take to fill the tub. Record their estimations. Then, fill the cups with water and invite each child to pour his or her water into the tub. Repeat the activity by asking children to fill and dump their cups again. Each time a round of cups has been dumped into the tub, offer children the opportunity to adjust their estimations. Record each successive set of estimations. If, with experience, children's estimations come closer and closer to the correct answer, point out this fact to them.

The Tomorrow Monkeys

*a Folktale
from Brazil*

This open-ended story describes the antics and good intentions of a merry monkey family. The repetitive language and structure help guarantee that children will quickly commit the tale to memory. They'll want to tell this tale themselves, again and again!

Fingerplay Start-Ups

Before beginning, tell children that they are going to hear a story that's written in a special way. Tell them also that, at the story's end, you will ask if anyone was able to discover the story's secret. (It can go on and on.)

This is a story from Brazil about some little monkeys who play along a river, the Rio Negro. **They play and play and play all day** beneath the warm sun and the blue skies.

And when the sun goes down,

the monkeys climb up the tall palm trees,

and the clouds roll in,

and the rain starts falling,

and the wind begins to blow.

It gets cold, and soon **those monkeys are shivering, shivering**.

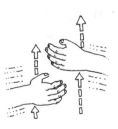

In the middle of the night,

the papa monkeys cry out,

"Tomorrow, let's build a house, let's build a house!"

**And the mama monkeys shout, "Yes, let's build a house,
let's build a house!"**

And the little monkeys agree, "Yeh-yeh-yeh-yeh-yeh-yeh-yeh!"

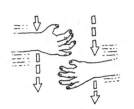

In the morning,

the sun comes up, the clouds roll away,

it's another beautiful, blue-sky day,

and the little monkeys climb down to play.

**And they play and play 'til one of the monkeys scratches her
head** and says, "Weren't we going to build a house today?"

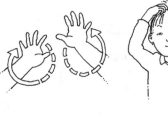

And the other monkeys say,
"Later for that, later for that!"
And they play and play and play.

'Til the sun goes down,

and the monkeys climb their trees,

and the clouds roll in,

and the rain starts falling,

and the wind blows.

It gets cold,

and soon **those monkeys are shivering again.**

And in the middle of the night,

the papa monkeys cry out,

"Tomorrow, let's build a house, let's build a house!"

And the mama monkeys shout, "Yes, let's build a house,

let's build a house!"

And the little monkeys agree, "Yeh-yeh-yeh-yeh-yeh-yeh-yeh!"

In the morning,

the sun comes up, the clouds roll away,

it's another beautiful, blue-sky day,

and the little monkeys climb down to play.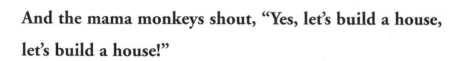

And they play and play 'til one of the monkeys scratches her

head and says, "Weren't we going to build a house today?"

And the other monkeys say,

"Later for that, later for that."

And they play and play and play.

'Til the sun goes down,

and **the monkeys climb their trees,**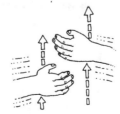

and the clouds roll in,

and the rain starts falling,

and the wind blows.

It gets cold,

and soon **those monkeys are shivering again.**

And in the middle of the night **the papa monkeys cry out,**

"Tomorrow, let's build a house, let's build a house!"

And the mama monkeys shout, "Yes, let's build a house,

let's build a house!"

And the little monkeys agree, "Yeh-yeh-yeh-yeh-yeh-yeh-yeh!"

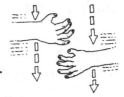

In the morning,

the sun comes up, the clouds roll away,

it's another beautiful, blue-sky day,

and the little monkeys climb down to play.

And they play and play 'til one of the monkeys scratches her

head and says, "Weren't we going to build a house today?"

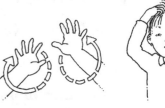

And do you think they ever build that house?

T H E   E N D

Talking About the Story

★ Discuss procrastination. Ask: Why do you think the title of this story is *The Tomorrow Monkeys*? Why did the monkeys think about building a house only at night? What kinds of things do you put off doing?

★ Then, talk about the weather. Ask: How does the weather affect our everyday lives? What are ways we prepare for changes in the weather? What happens when we're not ready for different types of weather, like hot sun, rain, or snow?

Across the Curriculum

MONKEY BUSINESS
Science and Art

Invite children to work in cooperative groups to find out about different types of monkeys that live in the rain forest. Have each group choose a different type of monkey and then prepare a poster that shows a drawing of the monkey, and a few facts about it such as its size, color, diet, etc. Display the posters on a bulletin board.

Then help students use paper plates and elastic thread to construct monkey masks representing faces of the different types of monkeys they researched. Students can then wear the masks when acting out the tale.

WHATEVER-THE-WEATHER STORIES
Language Arts

Help children make up other weather-related stories in which the characters don't anticipate impending inclement weather. Some possible titles include, "The Squirrel Who Didn't Save Nuts," "The Girl Who Forgot Her Umbrella," and "The Boy Who Wouldn't Shop for Snow Boots."

PROCRASTINATION POLL
Language Arts

Have children each interview one or two adult family or faculty members to develop a list of things these grown-ups put off doing. Combine your individual lists into one master list. Were any items repeated? Invite children to compile a list of suggestions to prevent procrastination. Make copies of this list and send one to each interviewee.

The Six Silly Cats in Calico Caps

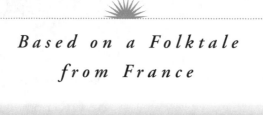

*Based on a Folktale
from France*

This is a story about six cats who are easily fooled by nature and are led astray by one another. Stories about fools exist in most every culture. The theme of being tricked by a water reflection, for example, can also be found in tales from Greece (Aesop's Fables), India, and Native American cultures.

Fingerplay Start-Ups

In this story, the six cats are represented as fingers, so the counting joke is presented in a very visual way. Tell the children that they are about to hear a story that contains a little counting riddle. Ask them to listen carefully to see if they can spot the riddle, and so they can figure out the riddle's answer.

Once, long ago, there were six cats—

three brother cats and three sister cats.

Let's count them!

One cat,

Two cats,

Three cats,

Four cats,

Five cats,

Six cats!

Everyone called them the six silly cats in calico caps because it seemed like something funny was always happening to them, and they always wore calico caps.

One day they decided to take a long walk together. The six cats put on their six calico caps and started **walking**. The cats had rarely been out of the village and they saw a lot of amazing sights.

When they came to a well, the six silly cats were not sure what it was. They moved carefully to the well's edge. Then they **looked deep down inside**.
"Meow!" they called.
"Meow!" the well echoed back.

The echo scared the six silly cats and **they went running!**

When they finally slowed down, one of the sisters was worried. She said, **"That meow from the well sounded just like us! Maybe one of us fell in!"**

The oldest brother scratched his head. He said, "Look, I'll count us and then we'll know if all six of us are still here."

The oldest brother started counting:

One cat,

Two cats,

Three cats,

Four cats,

Five cats!

He counted again:

One cat,

Two cats,

Three cats,

Four cats,

Five cats!

He counted again!

One cat,

Two cats,

Three cats,

Four cats,

Five cats!

Only five! You see, he forgot to count himself. He looked at his sister. "You're right," he said, "there are only five of us here. One of us must have fallen in!"

All six cats went running back to the well.

The oldest brother looked down into the well. He saw his reflection in the water. He turned to the others and said, "I see one of us down there. Give me a hand!"

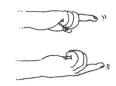

So, hanging on to one another, they lowered the oldest brother down into the well. Just as they were getting close to the bottom, the sister holding the oldest brother called out, "We're almost there!"

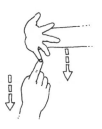

The four other cats got so excited they started clapping and cheering. Then all six cats in their calico caps went tumbling down into the well.

They were all tangled up in that well for a while. And all six cats got their calico caps soaking wet. Then they threw the caps up out of the well and climbed out themselves.

Once they were all back on the grass, the oldest saw the caps on the ground, and counted them:

One cap,

Two caps,

Three caps,

Four caps,

Five caps,

Six caps!

The oldest brother announced, "It was lucky we came back, because as you can see, we now have our six calico caps which means we are all back together."

They put on their caps and **the six silly cats in calico caps walked on**, whistling a happy tune!

THE END

Talking About the Story

★ Ask children to recall in what ways the silly cats were fooled. (The silly cats were fooled first by the echo and then by the reflection.)

★ At the story's end, how could the cats have realized that none of them fell into the well? (By asking one another who fell in alone.)

★ When and where have you seen your reflection? Have you ever heard your echo? What did it sound like? What makes an echo?

Across the Curriculum

REFLECTING ON REFLECTIONS
Science

Have children explore reflective surfaces. Set out a variety of materials such as mirrors, aluminum foil, metal spoons, plastic spoons, a bowl of water, construction paper, plastic containers, construction paper scraps, and wooden blocks. Which materials reflect light and which do not? Encourage children to explore and hypothesize about why some materials reflect light and some do not.

CALICO CATS STORY PROBLEMS
Math

Invite children to make up simple addition and subtraction problems based on the fingerplay. Begin by asking each child to draw six cats on a piece of paper. Then, have them each circle any number of cats to illustrate a cat problem, and then record their math story (in numbers and/or words) beneath the picture. For example, if four silly cats in calico hats climb a tree, and two more silly cats in calico hats join them, how many silly cats in calico hats are there in all?

Why the Moon Gets Smaller

a Folktale from Australia

The origin of celestial objects fills the folklore of every culture. This "why" story from the Aborigines of Australia attempts to explain the predictable pattern of the moon's phases each month.

Fingerplay Start-Ups

This story is especially fun for children because they can see for themselves how the moon changes size in the night sky. Ask children to listen to see if they believe this story could be true.

Long, long ago, there was a land where moons lived—**lots and lots of big, round, rolling moons**.
The land was green and beautiful
and the moons just rolled around.

One night, **one of the moons got rolling very fast. It rolled up a hill and into the sky. Then it crossed the sky.**

On the other side of the sky lived a giant.

This giant had a great big knife made of flint.

When the moon had crossed the sky, **he took it** and carved off a little slice.

Then the giant took that slice, chopped it into tiny pieces and threw them into the sky. They became stars.

Each night the moon came back across the sky and each night the giant waited with his great big knife.

When the moon got close, the giant took it down and sliced off a bit.

Then he chopped up the slice and threw the new stars into the sky.

The moon got smaller

and smaller

and smaller

until there was no moon at all left in the sky.

Then another of those moons in the land of moons rolled up the side of the mountain and across the sky.

The big old giant was there waiting with his great big knife.

This still happens night after night, month after month.

And that is why there are so many stars in the sky,

and why during each month,

the moon gets smaller

and smaller

and smaller

until there is no moon at all left in the sky.

THE END

Talking About the Story

Ask children whether they think this story is fact or fiction. Then talk with them to ascertain their understanding of what causes moon phases. If children aren't certain, or have never explored the topic, have them brainstorm a list of possible reasons. Then read aloud a nonfiction children's book that explains the science behind moon phases such as, *Where Does the Moon Go?* by Sidney Roden (Carolrhoda, 1992). Ask children to tell which explanation—folkloric or scientific—they prefer.

Across the Curriculum

MOON WATCH
Science

Supply each child with a month-long calendar page featuring blank date boxes large enough to hold small illustrations. Assign each child (or two children, in case of absences) to be in charge of recording what the moon looks like on a specific night. Have students circle their nights on their calendars. When students bring in their calendar page with their moon-phase drawing, their classmates can copy the drawing in the appropriate box on their own calendars. When the calendars are complete,

discuss how the moon changed. Do any patterns emerge? Have children refer to a book such as *So That's How the Moon Changes Shape* by Allan Fowler (Children's Press, 1991) so they may label their drawings with the correct terminology (crescent moon, quarter moon, gibbous moon, full moon). Point out to children that information on phases of the moon can be obtained from several sources, such as calendars, the Farmer's Almanac, and the weather page in the newspaper. Consider repeating the activity over several months so children can note the patterns of the moon's cycle over a longer period of time.

MULTICULTURAL STORY COMPARISONS
Language Arts and Social Studies

Share some other star and moon stories, such as, *Why the Sun and Moon Live in the Sky—an African Folktale*, by Elphinstone Dayrell (Houghton Mifflin, 1968) and stories about the origin of the Big Dipper, from Greek and Native American legends. Keep track of what is similar and different among the stories you share. Is it ever apparent how immediate geographic surroundings affect people's folk stories about how the universe was formed? If children show an interest, help them create their own celestial origin stories based on the forms your class explores together.

The Stonecutter

a Folktale from Japan

This particular tale is told throughout Asia with slight variations. There's even a version from Nepal in which a mouse princess, looking for a suitable mate, starts with the sun and winds up with another mouse.

Fingerplay Start-Ups

This story is circular in nature. Even though the main character begins and ends the story as a stonecutter, his perspective changes so he can now appreciate his position in life. Tell children to listen carefully, so that when you are done telling the story, they can tell you how the character changes and how he stays the same from beginning to end.

Once there was a Stonecutter.

Every day, **he cut stone from the mountain with his hammer and chisel:**

"Chuunk, chuunk, chuunk,

Chuunk, chuunk, chuunk."

Then he lifted the stone and put it in his cart.

He cut more stone:

"Chuunk, chuunk, chuunk,

Chuunk, chuunk, chuunk."

Then he lifted the stone and put it in his cart.

All day, every day, the Stonecutter worked, cutting stone and stacking it in his cart.

Every day, the sun rose and crossed the sky, shining down on the Stonecutter. The sun made him hot.

One day the Stonecutter was very tired and when the sun rose and beat down on him, he felt very weak. **"Oh, I wish I was as powerful as the sun. I wish I were the Sun!" he cried.**

It so happened a mountain spirit was nearby. It heard the Stonecutter and gave him his wish. **The Stonecutter became the Sun!**

"Oh, I like this," said the Stonecutter who was now the Sun. "I can see everything! I am the most powerful thing there is!"

He was happy being the Sun until one day **a cloud floated in front of him.**
"Hey! Excuse me, Cloud, I'm trying to see!"
The Cloud did not move.
"Excuse me, Cloud!"
The Cloud still did not move.
"Oh, I get it," exclaimed the Stonecutter.

"The Cloud is more powerful than the Sun.
Oh, I wish I were a Cloud!"
And, just like that, **he became a Cloud!**

The Stonecutter loved being a Cloud.
He could float across the sky, rain on gardens and
thunder when he was angry.
It was great until one day when he was trying to float
east and **the wind came at him.**

"Hey, Wind, stop! I'm trying to go the other way!"
cried the Cloud.
But the Wind did not stop.
"Oh, I get it," he exclaimed.
"The Wind is more powerful than the Cloud.
Oh, I wish I were the Wind!"
And just like that, **he became the Wind!**

The Stonecutter loved being the Wind.
He could go everywhere and see everything.
He knew he was finally the most powerful—
that is, until the day **he hit the Mountain.**

"Hey, move out of my way. I'm the Wind!"
But the Mountain did not move.
"Oh, I get it," he exclaimed.

"The Mountain is more powerful than the Wind.

Oh, I wish I were the Mountain!"

And just like that, **the Stonecutter became the Mountain!**

"Now I am truly powerful." And so it seemed.

The sun beat down and that felt good.

The clouds rained on him and cooled him off.

Then one day **he felt something at his foot—**

the foot of the Mountain.

"Chuunk, chuunk, chuunk,

Chuunk, chuunk, chuunk."

"Ouch, that hurts! Hey, down there, what are you doing?

Who is that? A Stonecutter! Oh, I get it!" he exclaimed.

"The Stonecutter is more powerful than the Mountain.

Oh, I wish I was a Stonecutter again!"

And just like that, **he was a Stonecutter again.**

And he went happily back to work:

"Chuunk, chuunk, chuunk,

Chuunk, chuunk, chuunk."

T H E   E N D

52

Talking About the Story

Ask children to comment on the story's theme of the importance of power. What does it mean to be powerful? Guide children to understand that there are many different ways people can gain power (e.g., with money, with muscles, with brains). Why do they believe it was important to the Stonecutter that he be powerful? Invite children to describe times they felt powerful, and times they felt powerless.

Across the Curriculum

EXPLORING NATURE'S POWERS
Science

This story offers a number of natural phenomena with specific natural powers. You can explore some of these attributes in class:

★ **Sun Power:** Place a thermometer in a bowl of water in a sunny window and another thermometer in a bowl of water in a shady spot. Check the bowls at regular intervals to see how the sun has affected the temperature of the water in each bowl. Discuss the reasons for any changes.

★ **Cloud Action:** Invite students to watch clouds to discover the shapes they become. Make a chart of the changing pictures students spot.

★ **Wind Power:** Cover empty coffee cans with construction paper and attach a number of crepe-paper streamers (approximately 12 inches long) around the edge of each can so they hang down. Attach a yarn hanger to the other end of each can. Invite children to use paints and markers to decorate the cans. Encourage children to take their cans home and hang them outside to help determine the wind's strength and direction on any particular day.

★ **Stone Strength:** Take students outside for a rock hunt. Back inside, browse through a geology field guide to discover the names of the rocks collected and to learn about each one. Tap the rocks together to discover the strength of each rock type. Which rock types are "most powerful"? Which rocks break easily?

SOUND EFFECTS
Drama

Inform children that in some stories the characters are enhanced or presented with sound effects (or music). Begin by listing the possible characters that might be depicted by sound: the Stonecutter, the Sun, the Cloud, the Wind, and the Mountain. Have children suggest different materials they might use to represent each one: stones clicking together for the Stonecutter; hands tapping lightly on the rug to represent the hot Sun beating down; soft humming for the still Cloud, etc. Then divide the class into groups, with each group representing a different story character. Each time a character is mentioned in the story, the group representing that character performs the corresponding background sound effects.

The Wild Cherry Tree

a Folktale from Mexico

This spicy little story is from Mexico. It's inspired by the foods common to this country, including onions, tomatoes, and chili peppers. In this tale, the foods come to life and are led astray by a tree full of tempting cherries.

Fingerplay Start-Ups

Tell children that storytellers often "spice up" their stories with personification. That is, they give human traits, abilities and personalities to objects or animals. Ask children to notice how this story uses personification to add a bit of fun to the otherwise ordinary situation of needing to fetch some water.

Once there was a little old man and a little old woman **and they were sitting at the table in their house.**

On the table were **a tomato,**

an onion,

and a chili pepper.

The little old man and the little old woman
needed some water.

**So the tomato rolled off the table
and headed toward the river to fetch some.**

On the way the tomato saw a cherry tree.
Oooh! Those cherries looked good!

**The tomato climbed up into the cherry tree
and started eating cherries.**

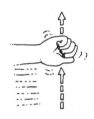

The little old man and the little old woman
sat at their table and waited for the tomato to
return. They waited and waited and waited.

They decided to send the onion.

**The onion rolled off the table
and headed toward the river to get some water.**

On the way the onion saw the cherry tree. Oooh!
Those cherries looked good!

**The onion climbed up into the cherry tree and
started eating cherries.**

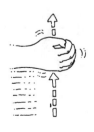

The little old man and the little old woman **sat at their table** and waited for the onion. They waited and waited and waited.

They sent the chili pepper.

The chili pepper jumped off the table and headed toward the river to get some water.

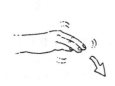

On the way the chili pepper saw the cherry tree. Oooh! Those cherries looked good!

The chili pepper climbed up into the cherry tree and started eating cherries.

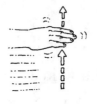

The little old man and the little old woman **sat at their table and waited.** They waited and waited and waited. They looked at each other, got up, **and headed for the river.**

On the way they saw that cherry tree. Oooh! Those cherries looked good!

The little old man and the little old woman climbed up into the cherry tree **and started eating cherries.**

There they were—the little old man, the little old woman, the tomato, the onion, and the chili pepper—all up in the tree, **eating cherries!**

It so happened that **it was raining up** in the mountains and this caused the river to flood.

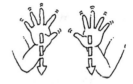

The river's waters rose higher and higher and higher.

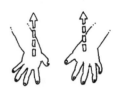

The flooding river pulled the tree right out of the ground and **carried it and all its passengers downstream into the ocean.**

The little old man and the little old woman and the tomato and the onion and the chili pepper **swam to shore** and walked back home.

The little old man and the little old woman **sat down at the table.**

The tomato,

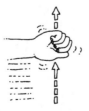

the onion,

and the **chili pepper**

climbed back up onto the table.

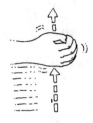 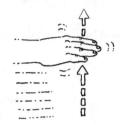

And do you know what?

The little old man and the little old woman
still needed some water.

THE END

Talking About the Story

Ask children to talk again about the
personification element. Ask: How might
the story be different if the foods didn't
"come to life"?

Across the Curriculum

FLOOD WATCH
Science

A flash flood occurs in this story, washing
away the cherry tree and carrying it to the
ocean. Help students explore the effects of
erosion with this simple demonstration: Fill
two foam meat trays with soil. Plant grass
seeds in one tray and keep them moist. After
the seeds have sprouted, place a book under
both trays to tilt them. Then, pour a cup of
water on both trays. What happens? The
bare soil can't hold on to water, so a lot of it
washes away. Soil covered with vegetation
erodes less. This can sometimes help
prevent floods.

VEGGIE PRINTS
Language Arts and Art

Have children use onions and chili peppers
cut in half and dipped in tempera paints to
create veggie prints. If children place prints
on large, thin sheets of easel paper, they may
use these decorated sheets as wrapping
papers for gifts. Children may also print
along the border of pieces of construction
paper and then use the papers to recount or
illustrate the story of *The Wild Cherry Tree*.

The Woodcutters

a Folktale from Poland

This old tale from Eastern Europe exists in many other versions throughout Europe and England. The story's theme suggests that though you may search far and wide, your very own treasure may be closer to home than you think!

Fingerplay Start-Ups

Tell children that the story they are about to hear involves dreams and a quest for treasure. Ask them to listen to the story and then be ready to tell whether or not they've ever dreamed such a "journey" dream.

There was once a group of woodcutters who lived together in a house on the edge of the woods.

It was a wooden house with a porch and a green roof. Behind the house stood a **huge oak tree**.

One night the woodcutters had a dream.
In the dream **they walked** along a dirt road.
The road went up over a hill, down the other side and **across a bridge**.

On the bridge stood **a guard wearing a red uniform with gold buttons and a tall black hat** with a golden eagle on its front.

In the dream, the woodcutters went under the bridge and **dug in the ground**. They dug until their shovels hit something hard. It was a chest. **They opened the lid.** It was filled with gold!

As soon as they saw the gold, they woke up. One of the woodcutters described the dream. The others exclaimed, **"Hey, we had that dream too!"**

But soon they forgot about the dream, and went into the forest to do their woodcutting. At the end of the day, they came home, ate their dinner and went to bed.

That night they all had the same dream!
. . . walking down the road . . .
. . . coming to the bridge . . .
. . . the guard in the red uniform with gold buttons and the tall black hat with an eagle on its front . . .
. . . digging under the bridge . . .
. . . opening the chest full of gold.

They woke up.

"I had that same dream again!"

"Me, too!"

"Me, too!"

"Me, too!" chimed in the others.

But then they forgot about the dream, and went into
the forest to do their woodcutting.

At the end of the day, they came home, ate their
dinner, and went to bed.

That night they had the same dream a third time!

. . . walking down the road . . .

. . . coming to the bridge . . .

**. . . the guard in the red uniform with gold buttons
and the tall black hat** with an eagle on its front . . .

. . . digging under the bridge . . .

. . . opening the chest full of gold.

They woke up.

"I had that same dream again!"

"Me, too!"

"Me, too!"

"Me, too!"

But this time they did not go to work. They decided
to follow their dream.

They walked and walked. They asked everyone
they met, "Do you know of a bridge with a guard in
a red uniform?" **People just shook their heads.** No
one had ever heard of such a place.

The woodcutters were about to give up when a
traveler said he had seen the bridge and the guard in
the red uniform. He gave them directions.

They walked and walked 'til they thought they
would drop. The woodcutters came up over a hill
and below them **they saw the bridge!** On the
bridge stood **a guard in a red uniform with gold
buttons and a tall black hat** with a golden eagle on
its front.

They ran down the hill, and started under the
bridge. The guard cried, "Halt! What are
you doing?"

The woodcutters told the guard about their dream
and their journey to his bridge.

The guard laughed, "You came all the way here because of a silly dream!? Well, this is the King's bridge and the King's land and you cannot dig here. So you may as well go back home."

Then the guard added, "You certainly have wasted your time. I had the same dream **three times**, but I certainly did not leave my post at the bridge to follow that dream!"

One of the woodcutters asked,
"What was your dream?"

The guard answered, "Oh it was silly. I dreamed I came to a wooden house on the edge of the woods. I walked past the porch and behind the house, where **I dug** under a **big oak tree**. There I found **a treasure chest full of gold**. It was a wonderful dream, but I stayed right here. And you'd better get back to your woodcutting!"

The tired and disappointed woodcutters **began their long walk home**. All at once they stopped and looked at one another. Then, without a word, they started running for their home.

When they got there they ran around behind the house, and **started digging** under **the great oak tree**.

It wasn't long before the shovels hit something hard. **It was a treasure chest!** And it was full of gold!

THE END

Talking About the Story

Invite children to share any dreams that they may have had—especially those that are similar to the journey dreams described in the story. Make a list of children's dreams. Next to each dream, write the names of children who have had those same dreams in common. Discuss the possible meanings of each dream type.

Across the Curriculum

PICKING PARTS TO PLAY
Language Arts and Drama

This story is great for opening children's minds to dramatic possibilities. Allow the children to choose parts from the story to act out. Encourage them to select parts you may not have readily considered (e.g., the treasure chest, the bridge, etc.). Whenever possible, encourage pairs of children to collaborate on how they might depict the story elements or make characters come to life.

TREASURE CHESTS
Art and Social Studies

Have each child bring a shoe box to school. Cover the boxes and lids with brown craft paper. Place the lids on the boxes. Create a hinged lid by first taping each lid to its box along one long edge, and then slitting the lid at the two corners that are taped to the box. Use a hot-glue gun (adult use only) to fix a decorative gold button to the edge of the lid to serve as a handle. Then offer children gold stick-on stars (or potato printers cut into star shapes and a supply of gold paint) so they may decorate their treasure chests. Invite children to collect special treasures (nature finds, tiny toys, small books, notes, cards, photos, etc.) that hold meaning for them. Then set a date to share the treasure chests in class.

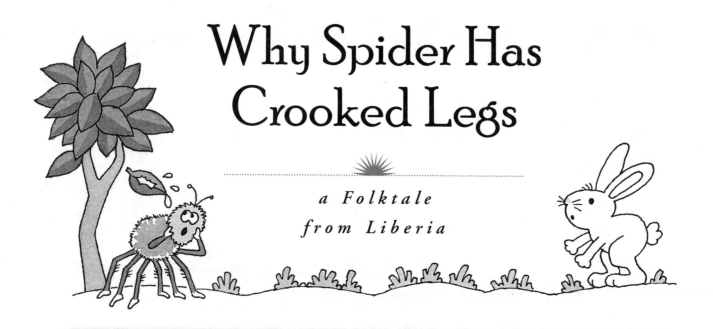

Why Spider Has Crooked Legs

a Folktale from Liberia

This humorous tale tells how greed causes Spider to wind up with crooked legs. Spider, often called Anancy or Anansi, is a favorite character in West African and Caribbean folklore. He's a "trickster" who never seems to learn that a trickster usually winds up getting tricked himself.

Fingerplay Start-Ups

Tell children they are going to hear a story about how spiders used to have straight legs, and how they came to have bent or crooked legs. Invite children to experiment with using their hands to depict how both a crooked-legged spider and a straight-legged spider might look and move.

A long time ago, **Spider had long, straight legs and ran about** with his body high off the ground.

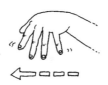

Spider did not like to work. When a drought came and there was not much food, Spider didn't even bother leaving his house.

Now **Rabbit** was not this way at all. She was a hard worker. **Every day she went out looking for food for her family.**

One day, Rabbit was hopping along when she smelled a wonderful smell coming over a wall. **She hopped up onto the wall** and **down to the ground on the other side.** There she saw a big tree with **huge petals.** The petals were filled with steaming stew! Ooooh! Did it smell good!

Rabbit sang gently to the tree, "Oh beautiful, wonderful, sweet-smelling tree, would you, could you, would you please **drop one little petal** down to me—just enough for my family?"

As soon as the song was complete, **a petal full of stew came floating gently down, down, down to the ground**, right in front of Rabbit's feet.

Rabbit thanked the tree, **took a little taste** and **hurried home** to her family to share the delicious stew.

After that, every day **Rabbit went back, hopped up onto the wall and over it.** Then she sang, "Oh

beautiful, wonderful, sweet-smelling tree, would you, could you, would you please **drop one little petal** down to me—just enough for my family?"

And as soon as the song was complete, **a petal full of stew came floating down, down, down to the ground**, right in front of Rabbit's feet. Rabbit's family had plenty to eat.

Now one day, **Rabbit ran right into Spider on her way home.** Spider asked, "Where did you get that steaming stew?"

Rabbit said, "Follow me!"

Spider followed Rabbit. **Rabbit hopped up onto the wall and over it.**
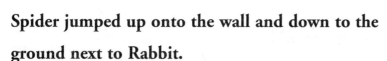
Spider jumped up onto the wall and down to the ground next to Rabbit.
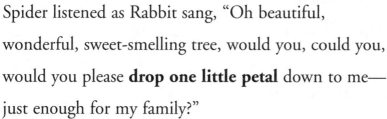
Spider listened as Rabbit sang, "Oh beautiful, wonderful, sweet-smelling tree, would you, could you, would you please **drop one little petal** down to me— just enough for my family?"

A little petal full of steaming stew floated gently down, down, down to Rabbit's feet. Rabbit thanked the tree. Now it was Spider's turn.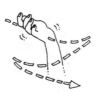

Spider did not feel like singing a sweet song and he was very hungry and wanted as much as he could get. He looked up at that tree and shouted, "Give me a great, big, huge petal full of stew! And make it snappy!"

Well, the tree did just that. **A huge petal full of hot stew dropped down from the top of the tree full speed and crashed right on Spider's back.**

Splat! Spider fell flat to the ground.

Rabbit pulled Spider out from under that petal and helped him back home. **Rabbit stopped by Spider's house every day after that** and shared a little stew until Spider was well.

Spider finally left his bed, but he no longer walked with those straight long legs. **Now he walked with crooked legs, just as he does today.**

Rain fell and the drought passed, and that strange stew tree disappeared, never to be seen again.

THE END

Talking About the Story

★ Explain that a moral is a lesson we learn from a story. Then ask: Why do you think the stew tree dropped a petal filled with stew down to Rabbit? Why did the Spider get smashed by the petal? What is the moral or lesson in this story? What if the tree had done nothing when Spider demanded some stew?

★ To help students explore the concepts of temptation and greed, ask: What food smells make you hungry? If you saw a plate full of that food (for example, cookies) what would you do? Would you take just one bite?

Across the Curriculum

EXPLORING JAZZY JOINTS
Science

This story "explains" why spider has crooked legs. In fact, crooked or jointed legs are a useful adaptation for spiders and other creepy-crawly bugs. Leg joints allow them to crawl easily over and around uneven surfaces. Have children move their bodies to discover which of their own body parts are jointed (knees, ankles, toes, fingers, arms). Ask: What do our joints allow us to do? What if we didn't have joints? Challenge children to try to walk without bending their legs, or to draw without bending their elbows and wrists. Invite them to write about how it felt to try doing these things.

COUNTING ON JOINTS
Math

You can develop some fun counting and adding activities using spider legs and joints. Display photos of spiders. Ask students to figure out how many legs a spider has (eight) and how many joints on each leg (five). Accept all reasonable answers and then ask children to explain their reasoning and how they arrived at their answers. Then, pose the following questions for students to figure out:

★ How many joints would two spiders have, all together? (80)

★ If there were 120 spider joints, how many spiders would there be? (3)

SPIDER STORY COMPARISONS
Language Arts

Read other stories about Anansi such as *Anansi the Spider: A Tale from the Ashanti*, by Gerald McDermott (Henry Holt, 1972); *Anansi Finds a Fool*, by Verna Aardema (Dial, 1992); and *Anansi and the Talking Melon*, retold by Eric Kimmel (Holiday House, 1994). Ask children to compare story elements to see how they are alike and how they are different. Have them read and listen to discover if Anansi is always a trickster. Is he always portrayed as a character needing to learn a lesson?

Sparrow and Crow

*a Folktale
from India*

This type of cumulative tale appears in many cultures. Typically, a disgruntled character is sent to one character after another in order to complete his or his appointed mission. In this story, Sparrow wants a pearl that Crow has taken. In an effort to get the precious pearl, Sparrow calls upon eleven different characters and demands that they use their special skills to help him.

Fingerplay Start-Ups

Before telling this story, acquaint students with each new action they will be performing with you. Then, assign one action to each child or group of children. As you tell the story, ask children to listen carefully for their cues to perform their actions as they are mentioned in the story. After a few retellings, children may want to take on the challenge of doing all the fingerplay actions on their own.

Once there was a crow in one tree
and a sparrow in another tree.
They both spotted something on the
ground and flew down.

Sparrow found a grain of rice and ate it.
Crow found a pearl, picked it up and flew
back to his branch.

Sparrow wanted the pearl and called up to Crow,

"Crow, Crow, give me that pearl!"

Crow said, "No, why should I?"

Sparrow said, "Wa-a-a-ah! Wa-a-a-ah!
Crow won't give me the pearl;
And I'm left here crying!"

So Sparrow flew to the tree and said,
"Tree, Tree, shake your branches!"

Tree said, "No, why should I?"

Sparrow cried, "Wa-a-a-ah! Wa-a-a-ah!
Tree won't shake its branches;
Crow won't give me the pearl;
And I'm left here crying!"

So Sparrow flew to the woodcutter.
"Woodcutter, Woodcutter, chop down that tree!"

Woodcutter said, "No, why should I?"

Sparrow cried, "Wa-a-a-ah! Wa-a-a-ah!
Woodcutter won't chop the Tree;

Tree won't shake its branches;

Crow won't give me the pearl;

And I'm left here crying!"

So Sparrow flew to the Queen.

"Queen, Queen, lock up the Woodcutter!"

Queen said, "No, why should I?"

Sparrow cried, "Wa-a-a-ah! Wa-a-a-ah!

Queen won't lock up the Woodcutter;

Woodcutter won't chop the Tree;

Tree won't shake its branches;

Crow won't give me the pearl;

And I'm left here crying!"

So Sparrow flew to Mouse and said,

"Mouse, Mouse, run up the Queen's leg!"

Mouse said, "No, why should I?"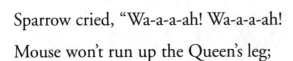

Sparrow cried, "Wa-a-a-ah! Wa-a-a-ah!

Mouse won't run up the Queen's leg;

Queen won't lock up the Woodcutter;

Woodcutter won't chop the Tree;

Tree won't shake its branches;

Crow won't give me the pearl;
And I'm left here crying!"

So Sparrow flew to Cat and said,
"Cat, Cat, chase that mouse!"

Cat said, "No, why should I?"

Sparrow cried, "Wa-a-a-ah! Wa-a-a-ah!

Cat won't chase Mouse;

Mouse won't run up the Queen's leg;

Queen won't lock up the Woodcutter;

Woodcutter won't chop the Tree;

Tree won't shake its branches;

Crow won't give me the pearl;

And I'm left here crying!"

So Sparrow flew to the dog and said,
"Dog, Dog, go bite that cat!

Dog said, "No, why should I?"

Sparrow cried, "Wa-a-a-ah! Wa-a-a-ah!

Dog won't bite Cat;

Cat won't chase Mouse;

Mouse won't run up the Queen's leg;

Queen won't lock up the Woodcutter;

Woodcutter won't chop the Tree;

Tree won't shake its branches;

Crow won't give me the pearl;

And I'm left here crying!"

So Sparrow flew to Stick and said,

"Stick, Stick, shake at Dog!"

Stick said, "No, why should I?"

Sparrow cried, "Wa-a-a-ah! Wa-a-a-ah!

Stick won't shake at Dog;

Dog won't bite Cat;

Cat won't chase Mouse;

Mouse won't run up the Queen's leg;

Queen won't lock up the Woodcutter;

Woodcutter won't chop the Tree;

Tree won't shake its branches;

Crow won't give me the pearl;

And I'm left here crying!"

So Sparrow flew to Fire and said,

"Fire, Fire, burn up stick!"

Fire said, "No, why should I?"

Sparrow cried, "Wa-a-a-ah! Wa-a-a-ah!

Fire won't burn up Stick;

Stick won't shake at Dog;

Dog won't bite Cat;

Cat won't chase Mouse;

Mouse won't run up the Queen's leg;

Queen won't lock up the Woodcutter;

Woodcutter won't chop the Tree;

Tree won't shake its branches;

Crow won't give me the pearl;

And I'm left here crying!"

So Sparrow flew to Water and said,

"Water, Water, put out Fire!"

Water said, "No, why should I?"

Sparrow cried, "Wa-a-a-ah! Wa-a-a-ah!

Water won't put out Fire;

Fire won't burn up Stick;

Stick won't shake at Dog;

Dog won't bite Cat;

Cat won't chase Mouse;

Mouse won't run up the Queen's leg;

Queen won't lock up the Woodcutter;

Woodcutter won't chop the Tree;

Tree won't shake its branches;

Crow won't give me the pearl;

And I'm left here crying!"

So Sparrow flew to Elephant and said,

"Elephant, Elephant, drink up Water!"

Elephant said "No, why should I?"

Sparrow cried, "Wa-a-a-ah! Wa-a-a-ah!

Elephant won't drink up Water;

Water won't put out Fire;

Fire won't burn up Stick;

Stick won't shake at Dog;

Dog won't bite Cat;

Cat won't chase Mouse;

Mouse won't run up the Queen's leg;

Queen won't lock up the Woodcutter;

Woodcutter won't chop the Tree;

Tree won't shake its branches;

Crow won't give me the pearl;

And I'm left here crying!"

So Sparrow flew to Little Mosquito and said,

"Please, please, bite Elephant's ear!"

And Mosquito said, "Okay,"

and started to bite Elephant's ear;

And Elephant started drinking up Water;

And Water started putting out Fire;

And Fire started burning up Stick;

And Stick started shaking at Dog;

And Dog started to bite Cat;

And Cat started chasing Mouse;

And Mouse started running up the Queen's leg;

And the Queen started locking up the Woodcutter;

And Woodcutter started chopping the Tree;

And Tree started shaking its branches;

And Crow dropped the pearl;

And Sparrow picked it up—
And smiled.

T H E E N D

Talking About the Story

This story has an ending that may satisfy some and not others, depending on their notion of fair play. Here are some related questions for children to debate:

★ Do you think the sparrow should get the pearl? Why or why not?

★ Have you ever found something precious that belonged to someone else? What did you do?

★ Have you ever been with someone who found something valuable? What happened?

Across the Curriculum

WORKING ON SCRIPT REVISIONS
Language Arts and Drama

Ask children to each choose a character from the story (or pair off students so they share a character). The teacher plays Sparrow and the narrator. The story can then be rescripted so that the different characters announce what they won't do. For instance, the Woodcutter says, "And I won't cut down the tree," and Mouse says, "And I won't crawl up the Queen's leg," etc. The children then repeat these lines and act out their fingerplay movements each time they appear in the story. Children might also wish to collaborate on a new story ending.

GROWING A STORY
Language Arts

Invite students to create their own class cumulative tale using the cumulative tales in the book as a model. (See *The Fly's Castle,* page 23, and *The Woodcutters,* page 59.) Create a class big book for this new story. A nice thing about creating a class cumulative tale is that it can accumulate with single additions from each member of the class.

Resources

There are many wonderful picture books of single folktales available. This resource list focuses on good collections of tales. They offer a range of stories that can be chosen to fit your curriculum needs. Collections also provide an opportunity to choose a story which speaks to you.

General

The Care Treasury of Children's Folklore, Brian Scott Sockin and Eileen J. Wong, Berkley Books, 1995.

The Maid of the North: Feminist Folktales From Around the World, edited by Ethel Johnston Phelps, Henry Holt, 1981.

South and North, East and West, edited by Michael Rosen, Candlewick Press, 1992.

A World of Fairy Tales, retold by Andrew Lang, Dial Books, 1994.

North America

American Tall Tales, by Mary Pope Osborne, Alfred A. Knopf, 1991.

Cuentos: Tales from the Hispanic Southwest, selected and adapted in Spanish by Jose Griego y Maestas, retold in English by Rudolfo A. Anaya, The Museum of New Mexico Press, 1980.

Cut From the Same Cloth, American Women of Myth, Legend, and Tall Tale, collected and told by Robert D. San Souci, Philomel, 1993.

Her Stories: African American Folktales, Fairy Tales and True Tales, told by Virginia Hamilton, Scholastic, 1995.

Keepers of the Earth: Native American Stories and Environmental Activities for Children, Michael J. Caduto and Joseph Bruchac, Fulcrum, 1989.

The People Could Fly: American Black Folktales, told by Virginia Hamilton, Alfred A. Knopf, 1985.

Central & South America

The Bird Who Cleans the World and Other Mayan Fables, Victor Montejo, Curbstone Press, 1992.

The Boy Who Could Do Anything & Other Mexican Folk Tales, retold by Anita Brenner, Linnet Books, 1992.

Caribbean

The Magic Orange Tree and Other Haitian Folktales, collected by Diane Wolkstein, Schocken, 1978.

Spiderman Anancy, by James Berry, Henry Holt, 1988.

West Indian Folk-tales, retold by Philip Sherlock, Oxford University Press, 1989.

Africa

Anansi and the Moss-Covered Rock, retold by Eric Kimmel, Scholastic, 1990.

Bimwili and the Zimwi, retold by Verna Aardema, Dial, 1985.

The Cow-Tail Switch and Other West African Stories, retold by Harold Courlander and George Herzog, Henry Holt, 1986.

Asia

Favorite Fairy Tales Told in India, retold by Virginia Haviland, Beech Tree, 1994.

Japanese Children's Favorite Stories, edited by Florence Sakade, Charles E. Tuttle, 1996.

The Tiger's Whisker and Other Tales From Asia and the Pacific, Harold Courlander, Henry Holt, 1995.

Middle East

Miriam's Tambourine: Jewish Folktales From Around the World, selected and retold by Howard Schwartz, Oxford University Press, 1988.

Speak, Bird, Speak Again: Palestinian Arab Folktales, retold by Ibrahim Muhawi and Sharif Kanaana, University of California Press, 1989.

Russia

Russian Fairy Tales, collected by Alexandr Afanas'ev, Random House, 1945.

The Sun Maiden and the Crescent Moon: Siberian Folk Tales, collected and translated by James Riordan, Interlink Books, 1991.

Europe

The Juniper Tree and Other Tales From Grimm, translated by Lore Segal; Farrar, Straus, and Giroux; 1992.

Norwegian Folk Tales, collected by Petrer Christen Asbjornsen and Jorgen Moe, Random House, 1982.

Seven Tales by H.C. Anderson, translated from the Danish by Eva Le Gallienne, Harper Trophy, 1991.

British Isles

English Fables & Fairy Stories, retold by James Reeves, Oxford University Press, 1989.

Irish Fairy and Folk Tales, edited and selected by W. B. Yeats, Dorset Press, 1986.